HUMAN BODY

HUMAN BODY

DOROTHEA DEPRISCO
& MARNIE MASUDA

Interior Illustrations
by Robert Roper

SCHOLASTIC INC.
New York Toronto London Auckland Sydney
Mexico City New Delhi Hong Kong

ISBN 0-439-20215-9

12 11 10 9 8 7 6 5 4 3 2 1   1 2 3 4 5 6/0

Printed in the U.S.A.   01

First Scholastic printing, January 2001

TABLE OF CONTENTS

Your body is an amazing machine. In just one day:

- You exercise 7,000,000 brain cells.
- Your heart beats 103,689 times.
- You breathe 23,040 times.
- You move 750 major muscles.
- You speak 48,000 words.
- You eat 3¼ pounds of food.
- You drink 3.0 pounds of liquids.

Your body comes equipped with many systems that work together. Not one of these systems can work alone. They all have to get along in order to function properly. Together, the respiratory, circulatory, skeletal, muscular, digestive, and nervous systems help you to breathe, stand up, move, eat, talk, learn, and think. The best part about this book is that you will learn not just the everyday things about your body, but the cool and amazing facts that make science interesting and fun!

- Did you know what the largest organ is in your body? Can you guess? Yes, it's your skin!

- Skin is alive! It's made of thin layers of flat, stacked cells in which there are nerves, blood vessels, hair follicles, glands, and sensory receptors.

- Your skin feels heat, cold, pain, pressure, moisture, irritation, and tickles *because* it is filled with nerves.

- There are 45 miles of nerves inside your skin.

- The skin's epidermis has two layers. The top layer is made up of dead cells and directly underneath that layer there is a layer of living tissue. The top layer acts as a buffer between the sensitive living tissue and the outside environment.

- Every month you grow an entire new layer of skin.

- You are likely to shed some 40 pounds of skin in your entire lifetime.

- A person loses 30,000–40,000 dead skin cells per minute.

- Right now, there are over a million dust mites — microscopic critters invisible to the naked eye — on your mattress and pillow, eating the dead skin cells that you shed last night!

- Your skin is very flexible, so that when you bend and stretch, you don't rip it open.

- Your skin is a great insulation system. It keeps heat in on cold days and releases sweat on hot days.

- As an adult, you may have more than 20 square feet of skin — about the size of a blanket!

- Each day, adults sweat enough through their skin to almost fill up a six-pack of soda cans.

• Your skin is very flexible, so that when you bend and stretch, you can't rip it open.

- Skin manufactures and oozes all sorts of liquids. Different types of oils (and even wax) act as your body's natural water-proofer and a protector against germs. They also make your skin softer.

- Ever been in the water for a long time and come out looking like a prune? Don't panic! Your skin is covered with its own special oil called *sebum*, which lubricates your skin and keeps it from getting soggy!

- A typical sunburn damages the blood vessels so much that it takes 4 to 15 months for them to return to their normal condition. Yet another reason to slap on the sunscreen!

- Breathe in, breathe out. In one hour you will have done that almost 900 times!

- You usually breathe between 12 and 15 times per minute, and you breathe in about 7 quarts of air every minute.

- Can you guess how plants help us breathe? We breathe air, use the oxygen in it, and release carbon dioxide. Plants absorb carbon dioxide and release oxygen.

- People tend to get more colds in the winter because they are indoors more and in closer contact with other people. When people sneeze, cough, or even breathe — germs go everywhere!

- Your body is hard at work when you sneeze. When you sneeze, your brain sends a message to all the different muscles involved. Your abdominal (stomach) muscles, chest muscles, diaphragm (the large muscle below your lungs that helps you breathe), the muscles that control your vocal cords, the muscles in the back of your throat, *and* the eyelid muscles all work together to create one tiny sneeze!

- Sneezing can send tiny particles speeding out of your nose at up to 100 miles per hour!

- It is impossible to sneeze with your eyes open.

- Your nose knows ... how to filter things out of the air before they make their way into your throat. What would happen if a fly tried to get in your nose? Well, inside the front surface of the nose are tiny pro-

tective hairs that catch dust and other ir-
ritants that would be harmful if they were
inhaled. The hairs would stop that fly and
make you sneeze!

- The right lung is slightly larger than the
  left.

- Kids breathe faster than adults.

- You lose about half a quart of water a day
  by breathing. This is the water vapor
  you see when you breathe onto a glass or
  mirror.

- Your lungs contain almost 1,500 miles of airway and more than 300 aveoli or air sacs.

- The surface area of the lungs is about the same size as a tennis court.

- Even if you can hold your breath for a really long time, you will never be able to harm yourself. Your body will make you take a breath eventually.

- Whispering is more wearing on your voice than speaking at a normal volume. It stretches your vocal cords just as much as shouting does. This makes the library and the ballgame equally hazardous to your vocal health.

- Hiccuping happens when your normal breathing pattern gets interrupted. Your diaphragm sends a big gust of air to your lungs, and at the same time, your brain sends a message to your tongue and throat to clamp down to stop the big rush of air.

- Did you know that if you didn't have a skeletal system you would be a lump of jelly on the floor? Not only do all of your 206 bones give you your own individual shape but they help protect all of your organs.

WITH BONES   WITHOUT BONES

IS THERE A DIFFERENCE? YOU DECIDE!

- Bones move with the help of muscles, which pull on bones so you can move. Along with muscles and joints, bones are responsible for you being able to move.

- Your skull, a series of fused bones, is like a helmet for your brain; your rib cage protects your heart and lungs.

- Your hand has 27 bones, but your face only has 14.

- The longest bone in your body is your thigh bone. It is called the *femur* and is equal to one-fourth your height.

- The smallest bone in your body is the stirrup bone in the ear, which can measure one-tenth of an inch.

- Although bones seem really hard, they're actually three-fourths water. This makes them light and spongy.

- As you get older, your bones grow and you get taller. You are likely to stop growing taller by the time you turn 16 (if you are a girl) and 18 (if you are a boy).

- You may think all bones are dead, but the bones that make up your skeleton are very much alive — growing and changing all the time, just like other parts of your body!

- If bones were not made of living cells, things like broken toes or arms or legs would never mend. If you break a bone, blood clots form to close up the space between the broken segments. Then your body mobilizes bone cells to deposit more of the hard stuff to bridge the break.

- Over half of your body's bones are in your hands and feet.

- You have more than 230 movable and semi-movable joints in your body.

- Ninety-seven percent of all creatures on earth have no backbone or spine!

- Humans and giraffes have the same number of bones in their necks. The secret is that giraffes have much longer vertebrae.

- Are you losing your bones? Well, you were born with over 300 bones. As you grow, some of these bones begin to come together. When you reach full adulthood, you will have only 206 bones.

- Joints in your neck enable your bones to pivot so that you can turn your head. Other joints, such as the shoulder joints, enable you to move your arms 360 degrees.

TOMMY'S TRIPLE-JOINTED NECK WAS OFTEN THE CAUSE OF TROUBLE IN THE CLASSROOM....

- The pelvis acts as a tough ring of protection, encircling the digestive system, the kidneys and other parts of the urinary system, and parts of the reproductive system. You can feel the outside edges of your pelvis by pushing down on your hips, a few inches below your belly button.

- Your skull is an amazing bone! All babies are born with spaces between the bones in their skulls. This allows the bones to move, close up, and even overlap as a baby is being born.

- Just about every bone in your body is made of the same materials. The outer part of each bone, which is smooth and very hard, is called the cortical bone. It's the part you see when you're looking at a skeleton costume at Halloween. Inside the cortical bone are many layers of cancellous bone, which look very much like a sponge. The cancellous bone protects the innermost area, the bone marrow, which is like a really thick, gooey jelly.

- Bone marrow makes new red and white blood cells. Red blood cells ensure that oxygen is delivered to all parts of your body, and white blood cells ensure that you are able to fight germs and disease.

- Ancient Egyptians regarded the heart as the center of intelligence and emotion. The heart and circulatory system were so important that they believed the brain to have no significance whatsoever. In the important process of mummification, the brain was removed through the nose and discarded.

- Human blood travels 60,000 miles per day on its journey through the arteries, capillaries, arterioles, and back through the veins and venules.

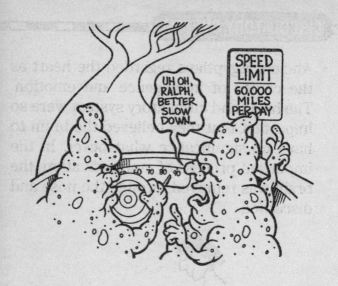

- The average human heart will beat three billion times in a person's lifetime and pump 50 million gallons of blood.

- Each square inch of your skin contains 20 feet of blood vessels.

- Did you know that if you took out your smallest blood vessels (called capillaries) and measured them, they would extend almost 1,000 miles?

- Your busy heart beats about 72 times a minute and 100,000 times a day.

- Around 8 million blood cells die in the body every second, and at the very same time, the same number are created.

- Red blood cells live for about 4 months, circulating throughout the body and feeding the 60 trillion other body cells.

- It takes about 20 seconds for a red blood cell to circle the entire body.

- The human heart creates enough pressure when it pumps blood through the body to squirt blood 30 feet.

- Every time you have a bite to eat, whether it's a four-course meal or a handful of potato chips, your digestive system works very hard to make sure you get the nutrition and energy your body needs to survive.

- Your digestive system carries food down your throat, into your stomach, through your intestines, and out your rectum, where it comes out as a bowel movement. This process can take anywhere from a few hours to two whole days!

- Your tongue is the strongest muscle in your whole body! Your tongue not only helps you talk and eat, but it pushes saliva into the throat to be swallowed — even while you're sleeping!

- On your tongue there are three major different types of papillae — two in front and one in back. Papillae help grip food and move it around while you chew. They also contain your taste buds, so you can taste everything.

- People are born with about 10,000 taste buds. But as a person gets older, some taste buds die. An older person may have only 4,000 taste buds! That's why some foods (especially spicy ones) may taste really strong to you but maybe not to your mom or dad!

- Taste buds on some parts of the tongue respond to different flavors. There are four main flavors that the taste buds can taste. Taste buds at the back of the tongue detect bitter flavors like black coffee. Taste buds on the sides taste sour foods such as grapefruit. Taste buds at the tip of the tongue detect sweet foods like cake and salty foods such as pretzels.

- If you gulp down your food or drink a lot of soda, you might find yourself belching. A belch (or "burp") is simply excess air in your digestive system that needs to get out.

- You swallow about seven quarts of air each day.

- You dribbled about 154 quarts of saliva before your first birthday. By the time you get old, you will have dribbled enough to cover two tennis courts!

- Your liver is your body's clearinghouse. It decides which nutrients your body needs, sending all the "good stuff" to the right places and all of the "bad stuff" out of you.

- There are 35 million digestive glands in the stomach.

- If you took out your large intestine and stretched it out on the ground, it would be about five feet long. Your intestine might be taller than you!

- You will eat approximately 50 tons of food during your lifetime.

- On the average, the American population eats 18 acres of pizza a day.

- Vomit is made up of half-digested food, spit, and gastric juices.

- Spit is a very important digestive substance. It turns your food into a sugary mush before you swallow, so your body can digest it easily.

- Food sloshes around in your juice-filled stomach for up to four hours before moving on.

- Bad breath can be caused by specific food (garlic or onions, for instance), or by the dreaded "mouth rot" — a buildup of plaque on your teeth that solidifies and begins to stink.

- Most people who have bad breath don't know it.

- Both the small and large human intestines together can grow up to 25 feet, but the average horse's intestines can be 89 feet long!

- If you get the hiccups, you can blame your own brain! It tells your diaphragm to jerk up and down really fast. Sometimes this happens after you've eaten too quickly or had too much to drink, but there's no one reason and no surefire "cure."

- "Farts" come out of your large intestine; "burps" come out of your esophagus.

- Greasy foods are the most difficult to digest.

- The human brain is an endless source of wonder for scientists, doctors, poets, and people like you and me. It's the source of our personalities, our hopes and dreams, our emotions, and our intelligence. It tells your lungs to breathe, your heart to beat, and your eyes to blink. It's the most complex and mysterious computer around — with built-in software updates every moment of your life!

- Our brains are growing! Three million years ago the biggest human brain measured a little more than 27 cubic inches (equivalent to modern chimpanzees and gorillas). Today the average human brain is between 76.27 and 88.48 cubic inches.

- Your brain has two sides or hemispheres. The right hemisphere controls the left side of the body, and the left hemisphere controls the right side.

- Some scientists believe that the right side of your brain is in charge of abstract thought: music, colors, shapes, and understanding "the big picture," but the left half is in charge of reasoning and logic — figuring out that tough math problem, for instance.

- Your brain gets more exercise when you're sleeping than it does when you're watching television. So instead of tuning in, maybe sometimes it's better to tune out.

- Your brain has a stem. Your brain stem controls all involuntary body functions such as breathing, digesting food, and circulating blood — functions you don't even think about but need to keep on doing in order to survive.

- Your brain resembles a slimy, spongy cauliflower split down the middle.

- The average human brain has about 100 billion nerve cells.

- The biggest part of your brain is called the cerebrum. It's the part that helps you think and reason. The human cerebrum is more than twice as large as your dog's or cat's. This is why you take care of them and not vice versa!

- Your brain is more powerful and complex than any computer ever built.

- Even when you're sleeping, your brain is working, doing all kinds of things. Your brain not only has the responsibility of learning all the things you need to learn in school, but it is the master of every emotion and feeling you have!

- Want to know why you get a "brain freeze" when you eat your ice cream too fast? When you lick your ice-cream cone, the cold ice cream hits your palate (the roof of your mouth). Then the nerves on your tongue send a message to the brain telling the brain to stop the flow of blood to your head. The blood vessels blow up, causing your head to hurt. But it really isn't your brain that hurts, it's the blood vessels!

- Athletes depend on the cerebellum to keep them in top form. It's the small area in the back of the brain that controls balance, movement, and coordination.

- Your brain weighs roughly three pounds, about the same as a carton of milk. More than two pounds of that weight is water.

- The hippocampus isn't a fancy prep school for big-game animals. It is the part of the cerebrum that helps you remember where you left your homework, how to get to your friend's birthday party, and where you were last night.

- Your nerves come out of your brain stem and run all the way down your spinal cord. These tiny threadlike "telephone lines" carry messages from one part of your body to another.

- Some scientists think that dreaming is your brain's way of sorting out important events of the day from unimportant ones. It's kind of like cleaning out your closet or your desk.

- Your brain is made up of millions of microscopic cells called "neurons." Each neuron has branches that connect to neighboring neurons. When you learn something new, the new information travels from one neuron to another. The more your neurons connect, the smarter you get!

- Your "motor area" is a part of the cerebrum that controls your voluntary muscles. If you need your body to perform a specific task — typing, tying your shoes, or chasing your brother out of your room — this part of your brain kicks in and helps out.

- The pituitary gland is a very tiny part of the brain (about the size of a pea!) whose job is to produce and release hormones into your growing body. This gland helps your body go through those awkward changes during puberty, the transition from childhood to adulthood.

- Brain cells die natural deaths every day. Drinking alcohol and taking drugs kill many brain cells very quickly and once a brain cell is dead, you can't replace it.

- Every cell in your whole body — from your skin cells to those cells deep inside you — sends millions of important messages to the brain every moment of the day!

- A concussion happens when your brain is jolted and knocks up against the inside of your skull. Although some concussions are life-threatening, others heal fairly quickly.

- Your brain is very active during the night! There are four stages in the sleeping process, and your brain controls each and every one. When you drift off to sleep your brain tells your heart to slow down and your body to get cooler. In the second stage, your brain tells your body to sleep lightly but to wake up if there's a noise or disturbance. During the deepest sleep phase, your brain tells your blood pressure to decrease. Sometimes people walk or talk in their sleep during this phase! The final phase is REM (or "rapid eye movement"). This is when you dream. When you are in the REM stage, your eyes start to flutter behind your eyelids.

- You have muscles throughout your entire body, even in places like your mouth and behind your eyes. Your muscles make movement possible, give your body shape and definition, and hold your bones together! Every time you move even the slightest bit, your muscular system must perform hundreds of small, important tasks. Exercising helps your muscles stay in shape, so they're ready to help you at a moment's notice.

- It takes the interaction of 72 different muscles to produce human speech.

- The human body contains more than 650 individual muscles (which are attached to your skeleton). Their main job is to provide movement for your body.

- Inside your muscles are tiny strings called filaments. These filaments are made of myosin and actin, two major proteins that help your muscles contract. When a nerve tells a muscle to contract, the myosin filaments grab onto the actin filaments and cause the whole muscle to move.

- Your trapezius muscles lie over your shoulders like a cape. When you shrug your shoulders to say "I dunno," you're using your trapezius muscles.

- Your deltoid muscles sit on top of your shoulders like shoulder pads and help you raise your hand to answer a question.

- The muscle with the longest name is the sternocleidomastoid. It runs down the side of your neck between your jawbone and your collarbone. You use it when you chew, talk, or bob your head to your favorite tune.

- The muscle that runs down the middle of your stomach is called "rectus abdominus." It connects the upper and lower halves of your body. It's also the main muscle you use when you exhale.

- Your obliques run along both sides of your abdomen. You use them when you use a hula hoop.

- The big muscle on the front of your upper arm is your biceps. It's what you show off when you "make a muscle." People who lift heavy things get big biceps.

BILLY DEMONSTRATES THE BICEPS MUSCLE
(LETTERS **A** AND **B**)

- Muscle cramps are your body's way of telling you to drink more water.

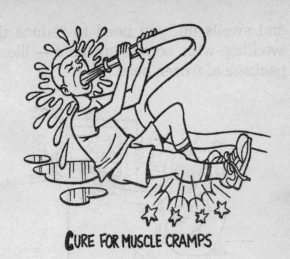

CURE FOR MUSCLE CRAMPS

- No one truly has double joints. Contortionists are actually able to stretch the fibrous tissues known as ligaments. Ligaments hold organs in place and fasten bones together. Ligaments normally restrict the movements of certain joints, but some may find that their ligaments are more flexible than others.

- Heat makes muscles expand, but cold makes them contract. When you "warm up" a muscle, you make it looser and less prone to injury. If a muscle gets injured and swells up, you need to reduce the swelling with something cold — like a package of frozen peas.

- Even though animals shed tears, humans are the only animals who cry when they are sad.

- The thyroid cartilage is more commonly known as the Adam's apple.

- The tooth is one of the few parts of the human body that cannot repair itself. If broken, it will never recover — except with the help of a dentist.

- The average human eye blinks 6,205,000 times per year.

- If you blink one eye, you will move more than 200 muscles.

- Women blink nearly twice as often as men do.

- If you laid all of the eyelashes end to end that you've shed in a lifetime, they would measure more than 98 feet.

- The ancient Egyptians shaved off their eyebrows to mourn the death of their cats.

- An adult human head weighs about 12 pounds or the same as a light bowling ball.

- Right-handed people live, on the average, nine years longer than left-handed people.

- Blond-haired people have more hair on their body than dark-haired people.

- Beards are the fastest growing hairs on the human body. If the average man never trimmed his beard, it would grow to nearly 30 feet in his lifetime.

- Your hair and nails are both very important parts of your body, and although they look different, they are both made of keratin, which is a hard protein. It is also the same protein that makes up the outermost layer of your skin.

- Your nails and hair are made of protein and they keep on growing and growing throughout your lifetime. In fact, your hair and nails will outlive you! They'll even grow for a while after you die.

- Your fingernails grow four times as fast as your toenails.

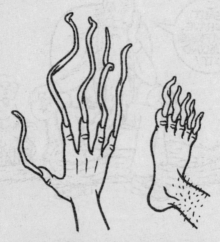

AFTER 10 YEARS WE SEE IT'S TRUE!
FINGER NAILS DO GROW FASTER THAN TOENAILS !

- In an average lifetime, a human will walk the equivalent of five times around the equator.

- If you sit and eat a whole bag of candy at once, then run to the bathroom and brush your teeth, you will get fewer cavities than if you ate the candy slowly, one piece at a time, all day long. So go ahead and chow down . . . but don't forget to brush!

- While you read this, your eyes are not moving continuously across the page. They're actually making tiny jumps — called "fixations" — from one clump of words to the next.

- Kidneys clean your blood. Each minute, about a quart of blood passes through your kidneys and comes out clean. Your kidneys will wash more than one million gallons of bad stuff out of your blood during your lifetime. Everything it cleans out comes out in your urine.

- Your appendix is the "do-nothing" organ. This little dead-end tube, which dangles about three inches below your large intestine, sometimes catches food particles and causes bacteria to grow. If this happens, it's time to get it removed.

- You have been hearing things ever since your days in the womb! A fetus responds to sounds even when its mother's ears are completely muffled.

- The human ear can detect the ticking of a watch from six and a half yards away in a very quiet room.

- As much as six percent of the world's population may experience sleep paralysis, the inability to move and speak for several minutes after awakening.

- According to a 1999 survey conducted by the National Sleep Foundation, of those people who snore, 19 percent snore so loudly that they can be heard through a closed door.

According to a 1999 survey conducted by the National Sleep Foundation, of those people who snore, 13 percent snore so loudly that they can be heard through a closed door.

Dorothea DePrisco worked in publishing for seven years before moving to the island of Lana'i, in Hawaii. She is teaching high school English at Lana'i High and Elementary in Lana'i City. She will be traveling across the United States with her two cats, Felix and Lucy, before moving to her new home in the Los Angeles area.

Marnie Masuda has been teaching for eight years. She earned her MA in English from the University of California at Irvine. She is currently teaching and living with her husband, Harlan, in Maui, Hawaii. Marnie is currently working on her first novel.